The NFL Experience

By David Boss and Bill McGrane

A PLUME BOOK
NEW AMERICAN LIBRARY
TIMES MIRROR
NEW YORK AND SCARBOROUGH, ONTARIO

NAL BOOKS TRADEMARK REG. U.S. PAT. OFF. AND FOREIGN COUNTRIES
REGISTERED TRADEMARK—MARCA REGISTRADA
HECHO EN HARRISONBURG, VA., U.S.A.

SIGNET, SIGNET CLASSIC, MENTOR, PLUME,
MERIDIAN and NAL BOOKS are published *in the United States* by
New American Library, 1633 Broadway, New York, New York 10019,
in Canada by The New American Library of Canada Limited,
81 Mack Avenue, Scarborough, Ontario M1L 1M8

Boss, David, and McGrane, Bill
  The NFL Experience
  1. National Football League.   2. Football—United States.
I. Title.
GV955.5.N35M34   1985   796.332'64'0973   85-8805
ISBN 0-453-00503-9
First Printing, September 1985
1 2 3 4 5 6 7 8 9
PRINTED BY DAI NIPPON, TOKYO, JAPAN

Contents

"We'll just play 'em one game at a time."

—*Almost any NFL coach in almost any given week*

Business as Usual

The game is like a seamless garment, with no true point where you can say "this is the beginning" or "it ends here."

The game is.

From offseason preparation, through training camp, through the preseason, through the regular season, through playoffs, back into offseason preparation.

It's ongoing. Like a river. Like its people.

You only know a few of them, players and coaches, and that's fair enough because players and coaches are our focus.

The rest of us labor to keep them in focus...and not just on those fine fall Sundays.

In March, for instance.

Little about March to smack of football, right? March is for baseball, and its leisurely emergence from hibernation. March is drive-time in basketball and hockey...the month when studied nonchalance gets chewed up and spit out by the steel jaws of playoff pressure.

March is a football month, too.

Down on one knee, the trainer selected a blade of grass for

chewing and gave silent thanks for the warm California sun upon his back. The trainer was visiting from Buffalo, where the March sun has less muzzle-velocity.

"You wanta try the hop?" he asked.

The wide receiver was bent over, hands on his knees, catching his wind. The receiver had torn up a knee nearly a year earlier, and the trainer had gone to California to check on his rehabilitation. He was working him out in a city park south of Los Angeles.

"No problem," the receiver gasped. He stood up, mopped  his face on the front of his T-shirt, and trotted to the far side of the field. On the trainer's "go" command, he crow-hopped across the field, turned, and hopped back.

Late in the afternoon, the receiver drove the trainer back to the airport.

"I'm doing pretty good, huh?" the receiver asked. He drove a beautifully maintained old Triumph convertible, and popped it in and out of traffic-openings at a speed that made the trainer occasionally stomp on that imaginary passenger-seat brake.

"You're rehabbin' better than you drive," the trainer grunted.

"Aw. . .you oughta lighten up, Pete," the player said. "Don't take everything so seriously."

"I take staying in one piece seriously," the trainer replied, "you should, too." He ran a hand through his hair, then half-turned on the seat to face the player.

"That's what this whole thing is about!" He had to shout to make himself heard over the wind-noise.

"This here. . .the football. . .is your business, and that knee is equipment that qualifies you to be in the business."

He could feel the car slowing by tiny increments as the receiver backed off the accelerator.

"You didn't just get dinged last summer, Flip, you almost got cleaned out. You come within an ace of totaling a knee, and there ain't no wideouts playin' on one knee."

"I know, but. . ."

"But nothin'."

Trainers aren't "lighten-up" types.

They get to work early and leave late and if they're lucky they marry women who can deal with the fact that they're not home on many of those nice summer weekends when the husband next door is out barbecuing for his family.

"You're rehabbin' your knee," the trainer went on, "but you got to rehab your head, too. You played lucky for four years, then you got unlucky. This summer, you'll go against guys who are younger than you 'n' have two lucky legs, not just one.

"I think you can do it, providing you sort things out and decide what's important in your life. If it's still football, then you better take it very, very seriously. It ain't fun and games no more, Flip, where you got a bushel of speed and talent and you can just wing it."

They were in front of the terminal, and it was as if there had been a transfusion of attitudes. The receiver's face was clouded, and there was a register of warmth in the trainer's dark eyes.

"Thanks for comin' out, Pete," the player said. He was looking straight ahead.

The trainer reached over and ruffled his hair briefly.

"You're doin' real good," he said. "Ahead of schedule.

"I never got hurt like you, but I think I know how hard it must be to come back. You're really showin' me somethin'." He grabbed his gear from the back seat and stood over the car.

"Thanks for the ride, and call me on Monday mornings. . . every Monday morning. . .or there'll be hell to pay!".

The scout was into the valley by nightfall, and clear as the air is out there, he could see the lights of Boise in the distance.

Signing the registry in the hotel lobby, he smiled when he heard the sing-song drawl just behind him.

"Big Donnie."

He didn't look up from his signing. "Hey, Chief."

Boise State had "Pro Day" the next day, when college coaches set aside time in the spring so the pro scouts can come in and weigh, measure, and time the upcoming seniors.

Beginning late in February, scouts work the land from south to north, going to Pro Days and spring practice.

They both were old hands. They'd even played against one another, back before the game got so big. They'd played and then coached, and now they scouted. Only stop left was a rocking chair.

That knowledge rode with them in dusty Buicks and Oldsmobiles—a man who is on the road a lot will tell you a big car's the wisest choice—through the mountains of Tennessee, on across the flinty hills of Kansas and the numbing uniformity of Nebraska, out west where the vastness leaves you in awe.

One scouted for a team from the Midwest, the other for an East Coast team. They'd both been on the road for the better part of a month, but their schedules hadn't crossed until they hit Idaho.

They had two beers in the motel bar, and then they ordered the hamburger steak dinner in the motel restaurant. Scouts and truck drivers eat about the same.

They were big, fleshy, sun-burnt men, both of them pushing hard on 60. They wore wrinkle-free synthetic sport jackets, open-collared shirts, and store-teeth, because they'd lost their original issue playing in a time when helmets didn't have facemasks.

"You hear about Red?" the one asked, turning a water glass in a huge hand.

"No."

"Heart attack. I run into that young kid the Eagles got workin' the Coast...hell, I can't recall his name."

"Fitch, ain't it?"

"Yeah, him. I run into him down at Stillwater . . . must be two weeks ago, now. Told me Red took a heart attack late in January down in Tucson...he's got a place there." Red was a scout...a scout of their vintage.

"He make it?"

"Well, hell, I guess he's gonna be all right...that's what the kid said, anyway. Course, I reckon it'll be a while before he gets back out...if he ever does."

The scout named Donnie shook his head. "Makes a man

think about puttin' it down, don't it?" he asked.

"Makes a man wish, anyway," the scout called Chief said.

For a breakfast meeting, it was getting heavy.

"I don't know that there is a perfect solution to the traffic-flow," the stadium manager snapped.

The fellow from the team was a middle-management type, meaning he wasn't high-profile, just vital. Middle-management types do whatever the high-profile types have neither the time nor the inclination to do: gruntwork that pays pretty well. Ask a middle-management type for his job description and he's apt to get fuddled. But take him away from the equation, and suddenly there will be a great many things that don't get done.

The team guy was having breakfast with three people who operated the stadium where his club played. Bitching and bacon. That's the kind of session it was.

"I'm not looking for a perfect solution," he said. "I'm looking

for improvement. We get calls and letters from fans who sit in their cars and wait forty-five minutes to get out of the east lot after the game. You have one gate out of that lot. You've got a good attendant ratio when people come in before the game, but half of them disappear after the game. The traffic at that gate is like a demolition-derby."

The stadium manager compressed his lips in a thin, unyielding line. The look was not pleasant.

"We don't get complaints from any other tenants. . .not like the ones we always seem to get from you."

The team guy blew on his coffee.

"You don't have any other tenants that draw the crowds we draw, Lou. None of them."

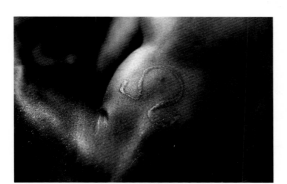

"That's our problem," the stadium manager growled. "When everything's full, some of the people are bound to have a delay."

The team guy set his cup down with a clatter.

"No, I'll tell you what your problem is, Lou . . . your problem is you're always saying, 'Hey, this is a problem for us.' You don't ever look at it and try to figure out a better way, you just say, 'it's a problem.' I'm saying, fix it. . . make it better! Of course it's a problem, but there's got to be a solution to it. That's why we pay you guys all that rent!"

He let his voice drop.

"Here's what I mean, Lou. If you go to the movies tonight with your wife, and if you have to sit in your car in the parking lot after the movies for forty-five minutes, waiting to get out. . . are you gonna go back to that theater again?"

The stadium manager was pouting.

"I don't go to the movies," he said.

The team guy turned his palms upward.

"I knew you'd understand," he said. "But get 'em outa the east lot quicker, okay?"

hat's the table for, Charley?"

The guard's eyes narrowed in apprehension. New devices in the weight room are to be viewed with apprehension.

Weight training, except for the charismatic few, ranks right up there with castor oil and root canals…nobody argues about their merit, but that doesn't mean you have to enjoy them.

"For you," the strength coach replied.

The guard sniffed. "I already got a table."

He circled the table slowly, studying it. He might have been a specialist, called in from ordnance, to examine a maverick bomb. He closley inspected every inch.

"Sure is a sturdy sucker," he said, grudgingly.

The strength coach nodded. "It has to be sturdy."

"Why's that?"

"So it won't break."

"Who's gonna break a table?" the guard demanded, his eyes losing none of their wariness.

"You might, when you jump up on it. . .if it weren't so sturdy," the strength coach explained.

The guard made a face. "Why would I want to be jumpin' up on a table?" he asked.

It was the end of the first week in March, and a cold wind on tour from Manitoba shouldered against the window glass,

causing it to creak in protest.

Depending on your finish, January is for purging, either in whole or in part. January is for sun-baked beaches, no telephones, leggy girls in brief swim-costumes and tall, cold drinks spiffed up with fruit slices and flower petals. It's a time for doing nothing.

February is for fun. Break a sweat, but no sweat, you know? Nothing too serious, though.

Three-on-three, half-court basketball, maybe, with a lot of

clowning around. Racquetball, or swimming, and a civilized approach to weights. . .and then everybody over to Boomer's for a pitcher or two of beer and updates on what has been happening to whom as the stragglers come back to town.

But March gets serious.

"You'll jump up onto the table for explosiveness," the strength coach explained.

"For what?"

"Explosiveness. Power. . .the blend of strength and motion. You're a good blocker now, but jumping up on that table will increase your power to where you can be a great blocker."

The guard's expression lengthened.

"How high is that, anyway?"

"Thirty-two inches. Eventually, we'll raise it to forty-two," the strength coach answered.

The guard shook his head. "I can't jump that high."

"Sure, you can."

"Sure, I'll break my damned neck!" the guard protested.

"No, you won't you're an athlete. You might bang a shin if you're not careful, but you don't even have to do that if you wear some padding."

The guard heaved a sigh.

"You sayin' we got to do this, Charley?"

The strength coach smiled. "You'll want to do it. We'll start gradually. . .at first, you'll jump just with five-pound dumbbells."

The guard's eyebrows shot up.

"We're gonna jump up on that thing, and carry weights while we're doin' it?"

"Sure. . .and by the time you peak in May, you'll be jumping forty-two inches and holding forty-five-pound dumbbells in each hand. We'll do three sets of ten reps."

The excitement shone in the face of the strength coach. The guard fixed him with an accusing eye.

"You got a cruel side to you, Charley...you really do."

The personnel director shook hands with his visitor and motioned him to a chair. Personnel directors are charged with identifying player talent. Talent comes from the colleges, from other pro teams, and from what is called either "the scrap pile," or "out there." Both phrases signify players who have been with other teams but presently are between jobs.

The visitor was a wide receiver drafted the previous year, but then cut by two teams. The personnel director had a mild interest and no illusions...he knew the receiver's skill limits, but he also knew you need fresh legs in training camp if you're going to get the passing game on-stream.

"I feel like I can make it...if I get a decent shot," the receiver was saying.

The personnel director folded his hands.

"Didn't you feel like you got a decent shot with the Jets, David...or over at Detroit?"

The receiver shrugged and made a bittersweet smile. "Well," he said, "I'm not trying to talk against them, but what it seemed like was...well, it kind of seemed like they knew who was going to make it before we ever got very far. Kind of like they were going to keep the veterans and the rest of us were there just to fill in."

The personnel director hated excuses. He was thrilled by success, he had come painstakingly to learn how to live with honest failure, and he hated excuses.

"About the only thing we could offer you is a chance," he said. "Probably no different than what the Jets and Detroit offered. . .I know their people, so I can say that. We'll go into camp liking the receivers who have been with us. You know why? Because they've got pelts hangin' on the wall is why. . . they've done it. Seems to me like it's wiser to judge a man on what he's done, rather than on what he says he's gonna do. New fellow, comin' in here. . .it's gonna be up to him to make our coaches like him better 'n' what we already got. The wide-outs we got now, that's what they had to do when they first come up."

The general manager stood as his secretary ushered a visitor into his office. The general manager came around from behind the desk, told her to bring soft drinks, and suggested they sit in the easy chairs where it would be more comfortable.

The visitor was one of the team's linebackers. He was strong, dedicated, fearless, and inestimably wise in the demanding ways of his craft. He also was 36 years old, and that was what prompted the general manager to suggest he fly up from Louisiana for an offseason visit.

They did the niceties for an unhurried 30 minutes. The linebacker talked about his family, about his sporting goods store, about a fishing trip he had planned off the Kona Coast. And, of course, about the weather.

After awhile, the linebacker smiled and herded the conversation back to where it was supposed to be headed.

"You didn't haul me up here," he said, "just to hear about Patty 'n' the kids."

The general manager removed his glasses and polished them on his necktie. He had a special regard for the linebacker. The general manager had played and played well in his time, and he knew about the purity some bring to the game in the way that they give of themselves. It would never have occurred to the general manager that he "loved" the linebacker but, in fact, he did.

He also knew that he was right.

"No, I want to talk about them," he replied. "I also want to talk about you, and about us, and about what's down the road."

The linebacker hunched forward in his chair. He rolled powerful shoulders and studied his hands with their scars and their misshapen fingers.

"I have rehearsed this a hundred times in my head," he murmured. "I've even said it out loud, to myself, drivin' to work."

He looked up, abruptly, and his eyes were bright.

"I know it's time," he drawled. "Shoot, Patty's been sayin' it was time since the boy was born, and he's goin' on three." He slapped his thighs, stood up, and walked to the window. From the window, he could see the practice field. The personnel director was out there with the would-be receiver, timing him at forty yards.

"Forgot my speech, is what I did," the linebacker said, smiling.

"I'm not looking for a speech, Tommy," the general manager said, his feeling for the player showing through.

"I've put it all down on paper," the linebacker continued. "I've plussed and minused. . . ." He scrubbed a hand through sandy hair that was beginning to show gray.

"I've got my health, more or less. . .the store's finally startin' to turn the corner. . .the kids. . . ." He shook his head. "You know, Jennifer's goin' into junior high school this fall." He said it as if that surprised him.

"Those are plusses." He laughed nervously. "Whole lot more on the minus side. Minus side's on the field. It all comes down to movin'. . .I can still see it, I know what I'm supposed to do, but I flat can't run with them backs comin' out anymore. Maybe I never really could."

The general manager studied a diet soda can.

"You could," he said, "and did."

The linebacker shrugged.

"It's just hard, you know. I was embarrassed last year, playin' in spots, rather than all the time. I knew I was still part of

it, but it's not the same. And I know the reason it's not the same is because I'm not the same."

"That's one thing about all of us, Tommy," the general manager said. "We don't stay the same. And there's nothing we can do. . . ."

"I think about goin' to camp again. . .I been workin' and I feel good right now. . . ." The linebacker picked at the hem of a drape, frowning. "But what if I went to camp and got cut?" His hand dropped. "I don't think I could deal with you havin' to fire me."

He turned back to the window. The field was empty now.

"Like I said, it's hard. I love the game. . .I just love the danged game."

Ultimately, only the game endures.

We, who are of it, tell ourselves that we feed off of it. Wrong. The game feeds off of us.

Other than pocket combs, coaches are as portable as anything you can think of.

You can be the best receivers coach around. You can handle your people right and improve on their skills. And you might even hit it lucky and coach a bunch of great ones.

But if your team doesn't have a runner...doesn't have the guy who can get the ball to the receivers...doesn't have the people to play...then it's just a matter of time until they hand you an apple and a road map and say, good luck.

Nothing personal.

Life in miniature. We start dying the day we're born ...coaches start getting fired the day they're hired.

It's not practical to fire all the players. Generals get relieved of command, but nobody ever fires the army.

Players.

They are the "stuff," really, of which the seamless garment is made. The rest of us are weavers.

Not just the high-profile types, either. All of us weave. In October, when you're aware of us, and in March. when you're not.

Do you know about breaking down film?

Film men do.

Would you believe breaking down every running of a given play for the whole season? And then breaking it again...and again...to where you have every running of that given play against a 3-4 defense, and another reel showing it against a 4-3 defense.

And equipment men. . .Lord knows, equipment men are weavers.

For the same reason the knights of old must have felt like their armorers were important to them.

Nobody is as close to players as the equipment man. He lives with them. He hears the bitches and the bragging. He knows the frustration and the fear and the fury that they know. The pressures.

It's fine-line work. The equipment man has to be close to the players. . .to where they're comfortable with him. . .but at the same time he can't sell out management or the coaches.

Teams have two layers. The top layer is players and coaches. The bottom layer—the one you don't see so much of—is everybody else. The only reason the bottom layer has for being is to support the top layer.

The 49ers couldn't win without Joe Montana, right? Right.

They also couldn't win without the bottom layer. They couldn't win without the people who are the system that enabled them to acquire Montana, for openers. They couldn't win without everybody from secretaries who care about their jobs to ticket managers and travel coordinators who feel the same way about theirs. They couldn't win without everybody giving their best to whatever it is they're supposed to do.

Owners own. General managers manage. Coaches coach. Players play. Scouts scout. Doctors doctor. Grunts grunt. Everyone has a role. Everyone is important.

Clubs trip over that theory sometimes, a fact that contributes to our having losers as well as winners.

There was a guy who was in our business, and the business was the better for it. He's not anymore, though, which is another example of how things never stay the same.

He used to say, "We have a system, and it works. The trick is, for all of us to remember what our jobs are, to do them, to have some patience, and to believe in the system."

The purpose of this book is to show us as we are, in full measure, and not just as you see us on Sundays.

We're a lot like you.

We're a business, and we have a product. Our product is the game. New-wave types among us call the product "entertainment," and say we're part of the entertainment industry.

I hope not. The game is more than that.

And in a lot of ways, our business is like yours.

We argue, we fight, we carry grudges, and we get bogged down in pettiness. We take ourselves too seriously. We have

regrets, and we worry about what lies ahead. We dream grand dreams, then settle for make-do. We make mistakes, swear we'll learn from them, and then we go right out and make them again.

We all want to win. Those of us who do, do so only after separating wanting from being willing to do the things that winning demands.

The difference is very big.

Being willing to win involves grubby, tedious, selfless, relentless attention to every detail, and never mind how minor or crap-shrouded some of those details can be.

The touchdown pass that left you gasping?

It was supported by a training camp menu, worked over until it was appetizing as well as balanced and affordable. And by comfortable buses and charter flights that leave on

time. By purchase orders and clean laundry and readable news releases—and all the other little details.

From star running backs to groundskeepers, our best have learned how to cope with their work and its demands.

It's really no different than any other business.

This is the story of the game.

An Open-Hearth Furnace

Ode to training camp:
How do I hate you?
Let me count the ways. . . .
Why do players work and sweat in the offseason, sprinting and lifting away hours they might give to the more pleasurable pursuits of life?

They do it to "load up"—to stuff provisions into a ruck-sack of self, to prepare for the trek.

Training camp is the trek.

Eat, meet, and hit. And do it twice a day.

Hell must have two-a-days.

Training camp is an open-hearth furnace where the players burn away flaws and impurities, where they strive to forge that elusive weapon, singleness of purpose for the season ahead.

Training camp burns away "Yeah, but...." and "What about me?"

The military knocks down selfishness and builds the well-being of the group on its wreckage. So does pro football. The pay is better than what an army private will see, and the food beats what's served in army camps. Otherwise there's not much difference in the routines.

There's a numbing sameness for the veteran. Robot-time. Wait for eggs-to-order in the morning chow line, and think gray, neutral, robot thoughts. Don't think about fatigue and fear and weariness and resentment. They will wear you down.

For the rookie, there's panic, constant panic.

Panic comes when the rookie realizes how much there is to learn, how much is expected of him, and how little time there is to show the fruits of his learning.

The result of all of this is pressure.

It's what prompts men who are friends away from this place to snarl and swear at one another, and, finally, to fight.

The sun never blinks here, and neither do the coaches.

You're new, you're a lineman, and you have this headache. Head-explosion says it better. It's severe. . .and constant.

You feel every cut, chafe, itch, bruise, and blister. Your muscles chatter in exhaustion. Normal swallowing became impossible 10 minutes ago, so your tongue just hangs there, hardening. You fight against loss of concentration.

And, just when you put all you've got left into running a play, your position coach jumps up in your face—so close you catch his spit—and his shriek would do a chain saw proud.

"Run it right, rook, or I'll get me somebody who can!"

The quarterback glares at you in the huddle, "Get it together, will you, rook?"

Your panic is a silent scream. And it never lets up.

God, almighty, I AM together! This is all I got!

After practice, dress wet to hoard coolness. Bush-whacked in the parking lot by autograph hounds. They don't know you. They just know you're big, so you must be one of them.

A voice tinged with laughter is following right behind you.

"Sign, rook, but keep movin'. Stop and they'll never let you go." It's the quarterback. He peels off toward the other dorm and flashes a grin.

"Hang in there. . .you're doin' good."

Supper. Pork chops, fries, sweet corn, coleslaw, strawberry shortcake, and enough iced-tea to fill your helmet.

Same coach, different voice. Relaxed, not a shriek. A smile, even.

"You're gettin' too high in your pivot to get out on the sweep," he says to the startled rookie. "Pretend you're runnin' in a trench on a battlefield, and you gotta stay low because somebody's shootin' at you."

Somebody is.

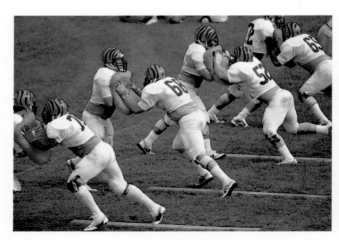

Football in the Twilight Zone

Damned veterans can drive you crazy....
   All week long, the regulars have been yawning and wise-cracking when they talk about tonight.

"Don't you be throwin' any of them boys around too hard, Ernie. I'd hate for one of 'em to land on me, now that I'm gettin' my legs back."

"Well then, you take an outside charge on Muñoz....I couldn't throw my dog that far. Big Muñoz, he'll ride you out to where he'll be askin' you for cab fare!"

But now it's here...the first preseason game, the first real step.

And the defensive tackle who had joshed about cab fare sits in front of his locker, head down, studying taped hands.

A rookie linebacker, dressed nearby, jumps when the defensive tackle looses a deep-throated, animal roar.

Across the room, a running back looks up and laughs.

"I believe Ernie's ready," he says.

Football in the twilight zone. They play the preseason games at six o'clock, not in the hard light of day, not in the electric starkness of a night game. Monet could have painted preseason games.

Usually, the crowds aren't as big as regular season. They're languorous crowds...do good and they clap, do bad and they don't. It's not the raw roar that will come later in the regular season.

All week long, the coach has been saying how the game will be meaningful because it will let him look at a lot of people.

In the locker room, after warmups, the coach calls them together for a pregame talk. There is an edge to his voice that the new men haven't heard before.

"We've been talking about how we got a lot to get done tonight, and we're going to...lot of you new people are going to play...we're goin' to get a look at you."

His eyes rake the circle around him and the color fans up in his cheeks.

"But I'll tell you why we're really here...."

"Kick their ass, is why...." A veteran's heavy voice from the back.

The coach nodded.

"You got it. We're here to win." His voice fell, but lost none of its menace.

"I don't ever want to lose," he said. "I don't want to lose tonight, I don't want to lose next week, I don't want to lose in January.

"See, winning's not like a beer tap. It's not something we can turn on when we want it. You win tonight, you do it one way...you got to want it worse than they do!"

Preseason.

Some will play well, some won't. Some will do even worse. They won't play at all, or they will play and get hurt.

Some rookie free agent will show something to make the coaches notice him.

Some vet will play poorly...blow a coverage, or, more likely, get beat just because his wheels aren't what they used to be. He'll still be cool along the sideline after they've put a kid in for him, but the fear will be there, a chill little doughnut in his gut, refusing digestion.

The injured won't show pain as much as they will show fear and frustration. Getting hurt means losing your place in line.

Not playing is the worst. The game wears down and a clean, un-hit uniform shines like some terrible badge.

Veterans get their work done early, then bide their time along the sidelines...a discreet distance behind the coach.

On the bus back to camp there are sandwiches, soft drinks, and beer in a darkness jarred by competing ghetto-blasters.

The ones who didn't play sit by themselves, not ignored so much as withdrawn. We die alone.

It isn't an easy business.

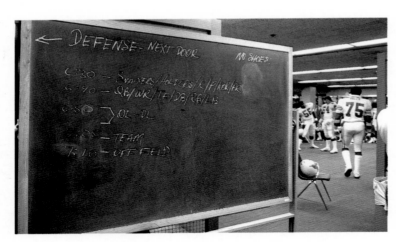

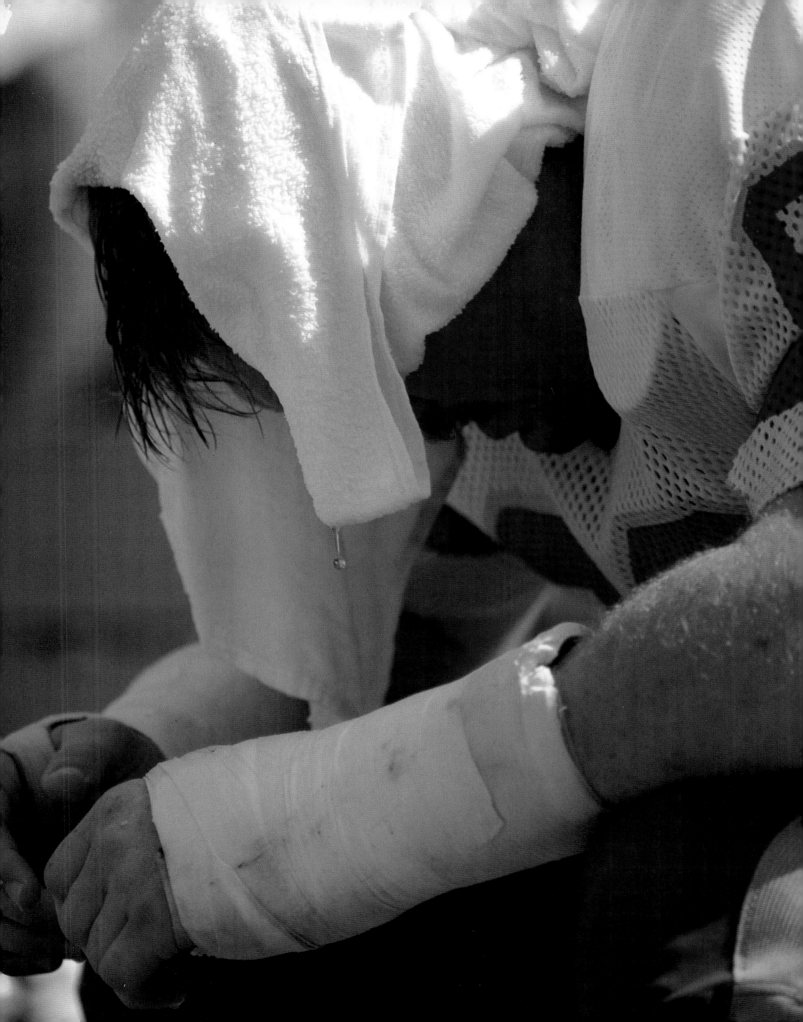

The March
Is a Long One

A measured stride....

If you strive for any one thing during the regular season, that's it. Pace. Consistency. A steady, resolute cadence.

All you really know going in, is that you don't know much about what's going to happen over the long season.

There's 16 games...you know about 16 games...all different...all difficult.

You know some of them will have more impact than others. Games within your division are two-pointers.

You know there will be days when the chemistry's better than it is others...no matter, you've got to play over the blahs.

You know there will be injuries. That position you laughed and scratched about in training camp...back when you had three good ones battling for the same job...can come up naked in November when it's time to go to the whip. That's when smoldering conversations take place.

Coach: "Hell, I never liked him when he was at Green Bay. I'm looking for a man-cover guy, not some damned tap dancer!"

Personnel director: "Coach, if he could cover, he wouldn't be on the scrap-pile. I know what you want! What I'm telling you about is what's available."

You plaster and patch and make do.

And you never stop teaching.

The defensive coordinator ignores the cold pizza and tamps new tobacco into his pipe. The middle linebacker chews steadily, ignoring the fact that the pizza is cold and virtually tasteless.

"That's what I mean, damnit."

The projector chitters in reverse, resetting the play. Tuesday night...supper-time, in the real world. On the screen, a celluloid guard collides with the linebacker, and a running back scampers by the collision for a big gain.

"Sold yourself too cheap," the coach grunts. "Now, you probably gave that guard one hell of a headache, but I can find me a hundred guys who'll do a head-on, then crash and burn. That's not what I want...that's not your job! You're the damned boss out there! You play off that guard, you read through him, and you go to the ball...always, to the ball."

A measured stride....

Get too intent on a fast start, and you can burn out before you get a hard freeze. Get too intent on laying back...saving it all for the finish...and they'll go ahead and finish without you.

If the unit...the team...maintains that measured stride, it does so because it is made up of people who do.

Play corner for 16 games, and you know one thing...Fouts or Marino or Lomax or one of those guys is going to burn the numbers right off your front.

No pain, no gain.

And the march is a long one.

Players store up hurts like a squirrel stores up nuts for winter...not that you want to, but what else is there to do with them?

A front-office type passes the trainer in the hall in late November.

"How are they, Bobby?" he asks.

"Hurt."

"All of 'em!" The trainer doesn't hide his anger. "We've played thirteen games...how the hell do you expect them to feel?"

They begin the march with grand design, and with shiny new vehicles-of-team. They chug into December with bald tires and most of the chrome knocked off.

And you know that's going to happen before it starts.

"You put one foot in front of the other," says the defensive end, "and your 'thinker' just kind of quits running. And that's probably good. You can see this light up ahead. You just hope it's the end of the tunnel, and not an oncomin' train."

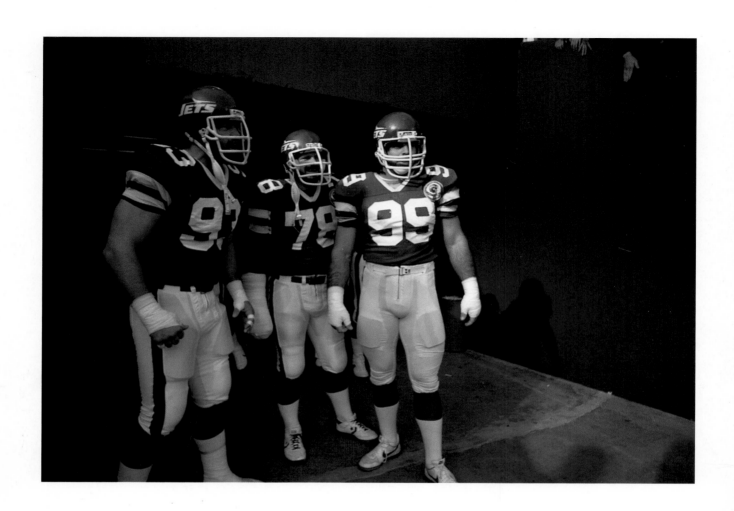

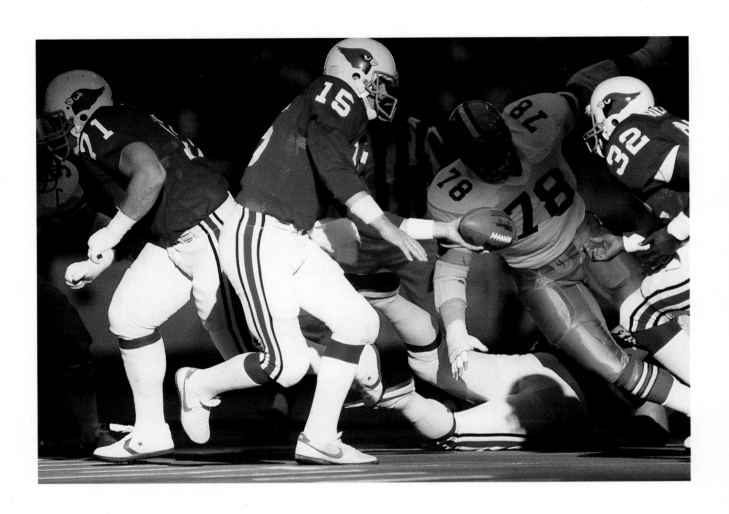

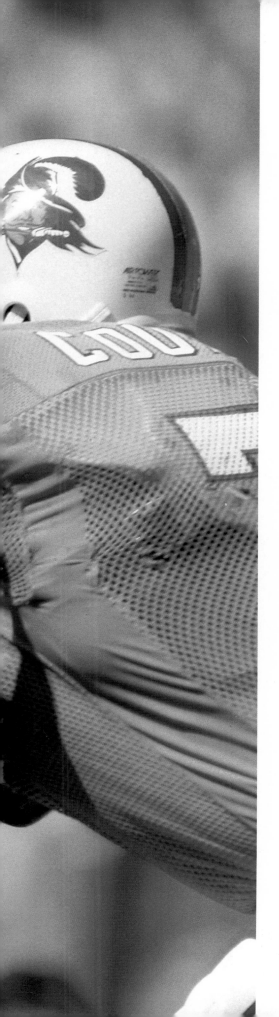

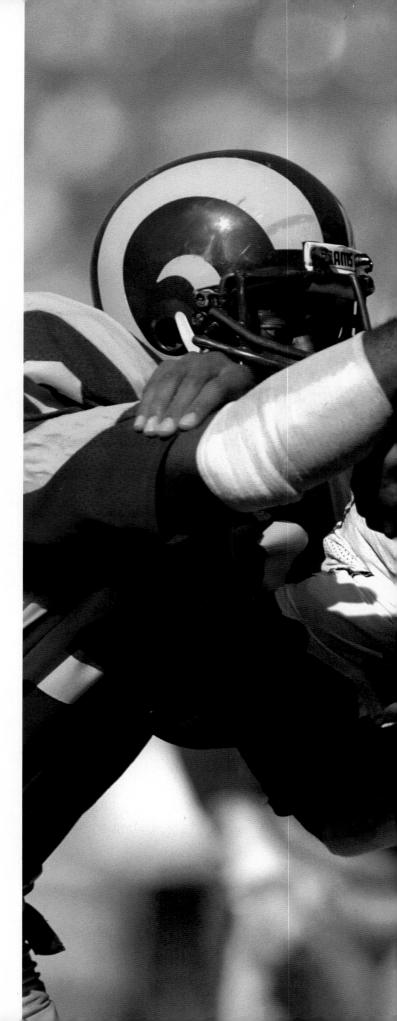

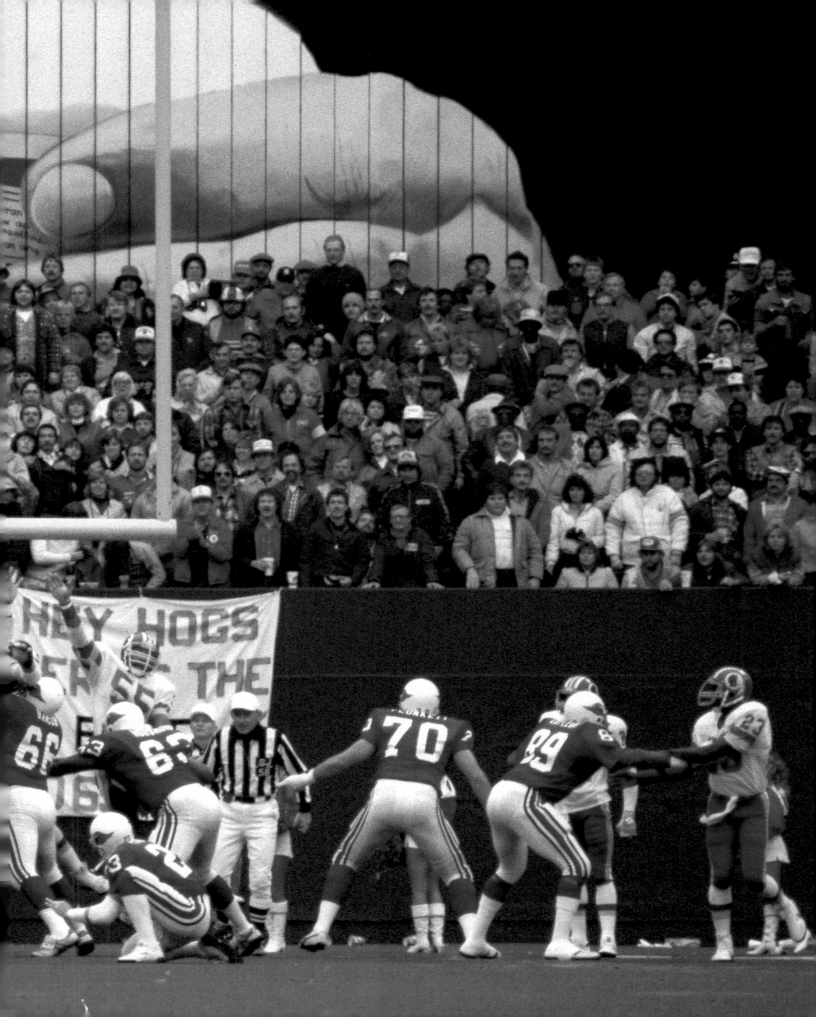

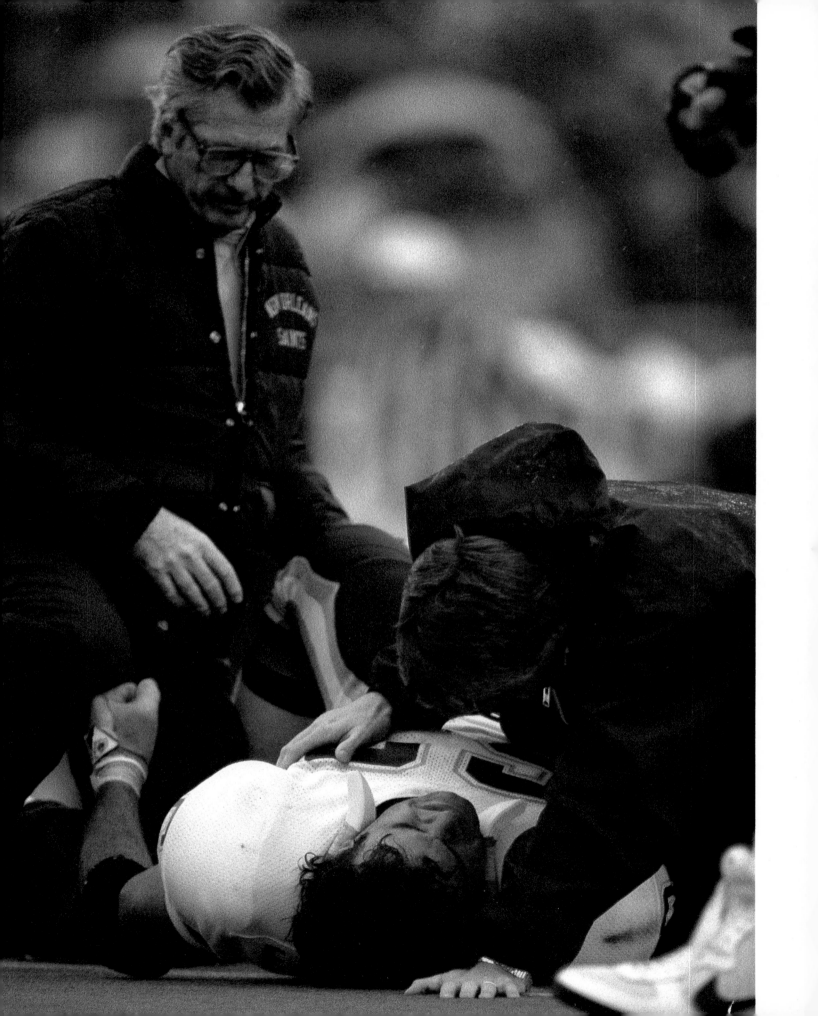

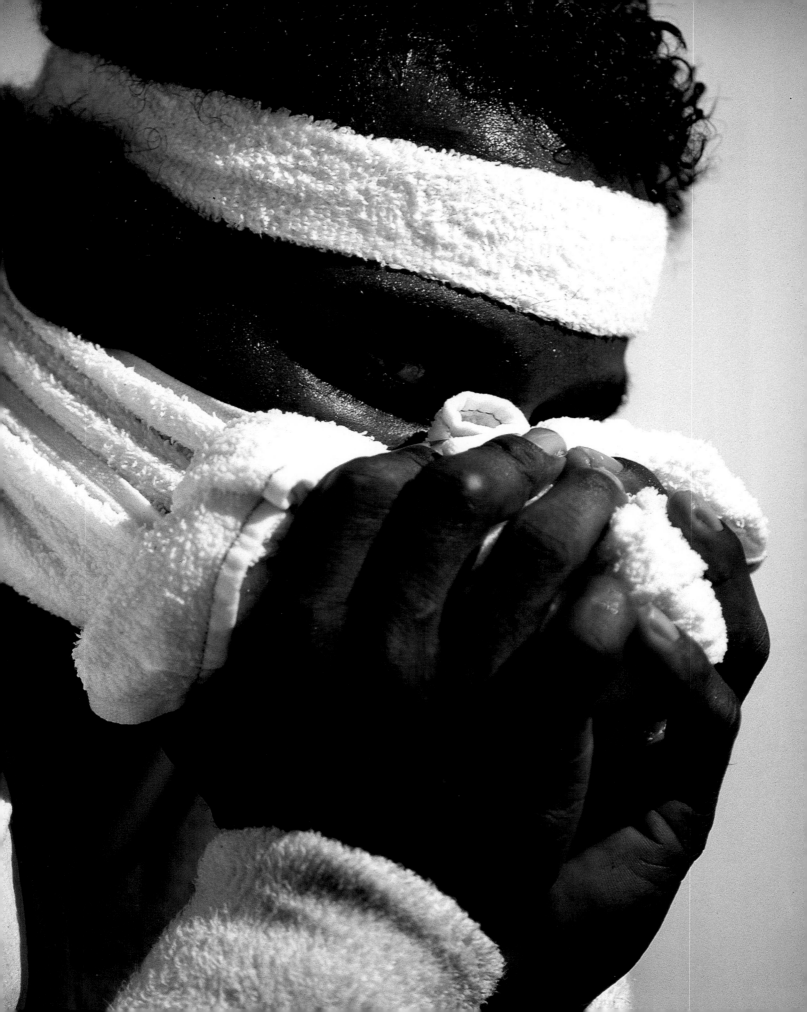

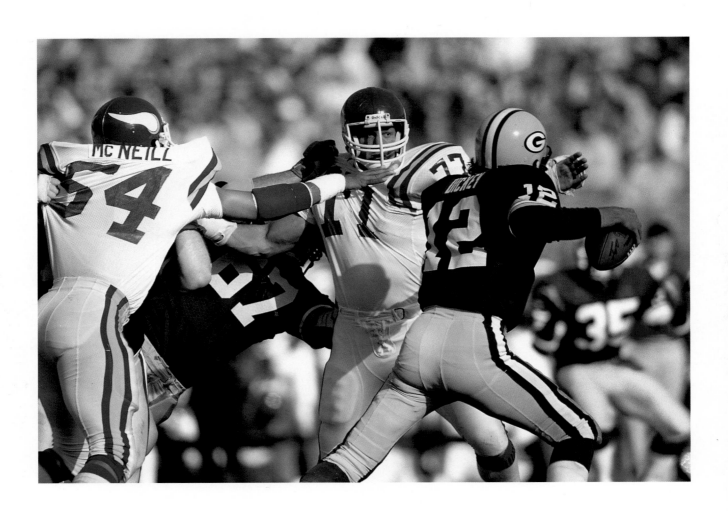

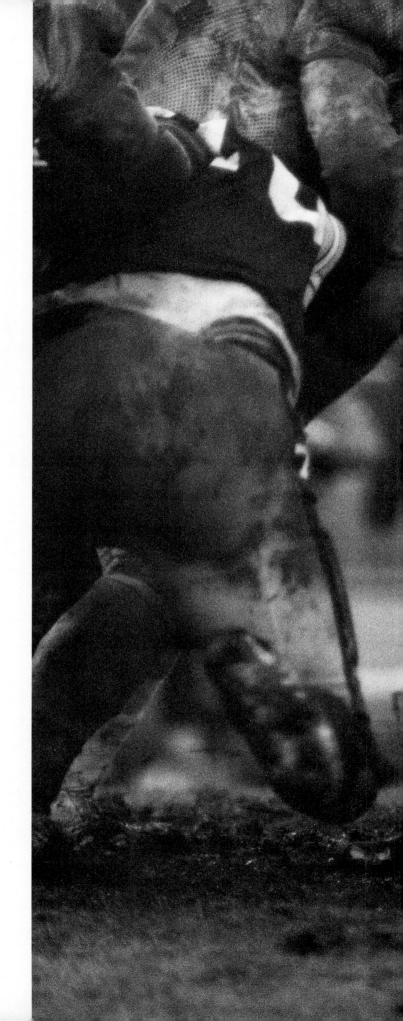

They've Taken Away the Net

If the regular season were a painting, it might be done in harmonious pastels...subtle, flowing, with a continuity of line.

Postseason is done in jagged black and white, stark and angry...as if pots of paint were hurled onto the canvas.

You go 14-2 in the regular season. You can laugh and win in your division and have the folks from Big Sandy to Muleshoe just tickled pink with the way you're carrying on.

But make one mistake. Mishandle one punt in a fine, freezing rain, or let Lofton turn you around and get behind you on an out-and-up...and they'll put a fork in you, baby, because you'll be done.

Nobody owes you another Sunday in the tournament. You either do it...or sit home with your rationalizations and watch the winners like everybody else.

You must deal with the shock value first.

You slog through the regular season in a rut of your own making. To get you to the tournament, it had to be the right kind of rut.

You clinched your division with three weeks to go and it was nice, but...hey, this is a new season.

Shock leads to impact...the realization that you're still up there on the wire, balancing, but now they've taken away the net. One misstep....

A veteran says, "We're treating it like it was just another game."

Sometimes veterans lie.

One body of opinion holds that watching football practice is almost as exciting as watching paint dry.

Until the playoffs.

If it's right, watching a team practice for the playoffs is electric. It doesn't matter that it's seven-on-seven and not game day. Receivers don't just come out of their turns, they explode. And when they do, the ball is there, waiting, hung as true as if the quarterback were using a plumb-bob.

This divisional playoff team went on defense first...got pushed back some, but eventually forced a punt.

On the next series, the first offensive play was a simple little quick opener inside right tackle. The line came off as one man, crisp as new money. The ball carrier didn't just run, he exploded into the hole. The play went for eight yards.

On the sideline, the coach felt a surge. He shouted at the backfield coach, and he had a fierce grin.

"I'm not sure how we're gonna do it," he said, "but we're gonna win this damned game. I know it!"

They did.

Afterwards, in the locker room, the coach called them together before the press got in. Where he couldn't see grins, he could see tears...or both.

His voice was so hoarse that the players had to strain to hear him.

"Fellas...." His arm flopped. He was fresh out of gestures, "this is why I been on you since the first day of camp." His voice rose, and so did the color in his face.

"For right now, and for the feeling every one of us has! Now you know...you don't think or hope, you know." He shrugged and smiled. "This is what it's all about."

They lost the next week...got to the Super Bowl doorstep and had the rug snapped out from under their feet. But they had got that far.

Afterwards, in the locker room, the coach stood on a little platform made of new, raw lumber. He faced a hundred newsmen, squinting against TV lights.

"I'd say something profound if I could, but I can't. We got beat...."

Quite a bit later, after the newsmen had left, the coach went off by himself into a little side room. He leaned his forehead against a cool cement wall.

It had come and gone so quickly.

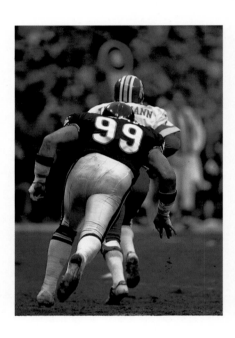

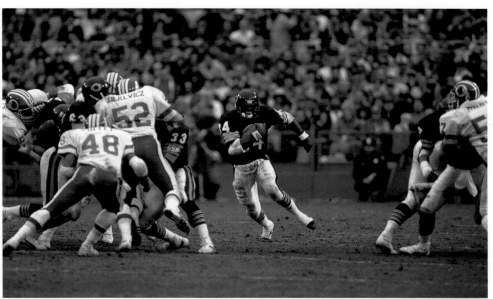

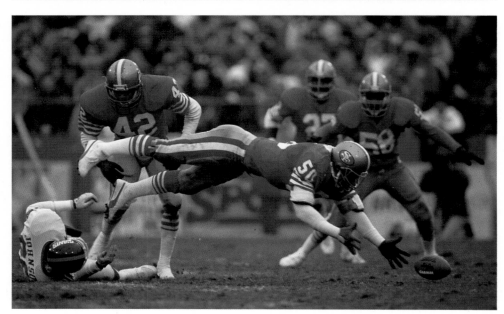

Even Offensive Linemen Get Interviewed

"**W**here's Sri Lanka?"

"Hmm?" The kicker kept on reading Ludlum.

"Where's Sri Lanka at?"

The kicker grimaced over his book.

"Where's Sri Lanka question mark. . .not where's Sri Lanka at." He set the book down. "Who am I, Rand-McNally? How the hell do I know where Sri Lanka is?"

"That's really something," the punter murmured almost to himself.

"What's that?"

"The announcer named places around the world where the game will be on television. Sri Lanka's one of them."

The kicker grunted, returning to Ludlum.

"Well, you wave to 'em," the kicker said, "and I'll try to find out how you say 'Hi' in Sri Lankese."

The thing is, the game's the same. There'll be great plays and bonehead plays and a lot more that are neither.

But there's so much attention. Thousands of newsmen hover before, during, and after the fact, and millions upon millions watch and listen via radio and television.

Even offensive linemen get interviewed.

At the Thursday press conference, the last chance for media-types to visit coaches and players before the game, a large guard takes the one open seat at a table with his name on it. The other seats are occupied by reporters, with their tape-recorders.

The guard smiles.

"Good morning, gentlemen. . .how may I bore you today?"

Nearby, a long-time linebacker holds his audience with a remarkable tale about a trip through a South American jungle where he was involved in an automobile accident.

"It sounds terrible," said a female reporter. "I can't imagine how you ever managed to live through it."

The linebacker fixed her with mystic blue eyes and a straight face.

"Oh," he said. "I didn't."

Salvation rests behind private barricades.

"I know there are a lot of distractions," the coach told his team. "It will help to remember this. . .I'm still me, you're still you, and what we have to do on Sunday is still what we've done before."

Sunday, after warmups, he talked to them again in the locker room.

"Some of you have been in this game for many years, some of you are new to it, but all of you have one thing in common. At some point, you came into the game because there was something in it that appealed to you, something you enjoyed.

"Don't forget that. I don't have any brilliant message for you. You're healthy, you're well-prepared, you have an opportunity most players will never have."

He stood for a long moment, studying the faces in front of him. He spoke to a receiver who was handsome, but garish now, with black grease daubed across his cheeks.

"Back in camp, Steve. . .what did I say was the one thing we had to remember?"

"You said we shouldn't be afraid to fail . . .said if we were afraid of failure, we'd fail."

"That still goes," the coach said.

He shrugged, and smiled at them. "So let's go do it."

After the game, in the interview area, the winning quarterback smiled at the bedlam.

"It really wasn't any different," he said. "I know that sounds phony, but it's true. I thought we all were a little brittle the first time we had the ball, but we got together after that and talked it out. The next time we went out, everything was fine."

The losing coach spoke to a much smaller audience in a quiet room.

"Disappointed, yes, embarrassed, no. It isn't easy, but sometimes you have to admit that the other team did better than you did. That happened today."

It always does.

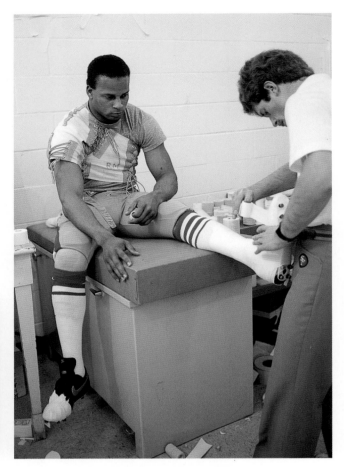

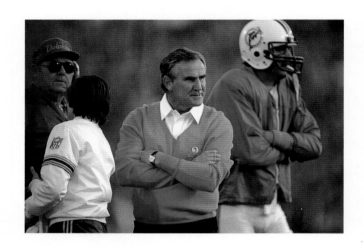

Notes on the Photographs

When National Football League photographers were told a year and a half ago that this book would be published, their response was gratifying in its enthusiasm and completeness.

The photographers were asked to document on film the game of professional football, to portray the game from the perspective of the coaches and players who experience it, day-by-day, for six consecutive months.

The photographers' personal involvement was critical to the success of the project. It shows in the images that fill the pages of this book.

The photographs published here represent the subjective decisions of the editor. Relatively few pictures were chosen, though many images were reviewed. So many in fact, that another book, equally powerful, could be produced.

In addition to the photographers, thanks also are due Glen Iwasaki for his precision and judgment in designing these pages, to Jere Wright and Jim Chaffin for the accurate production, and to Tina Thompson for the supervision of the printing processes.

Page 8 / Ross Lewis
Winter light beckons a solitary figure down a stadium tunnel for an afternoon workout.

Page 10 / Jim Chaffin
Rams linebacker Carl Ekern, a nine-year veteran, works out on the Nautilus equipment at the team's Anaheim, California, complex.

Page 12 / Herb Weitman
On a biting cold February day in Dallas, top college prospects are brought together for a series of trials before the critical eyes of professional personnel directors and coaches.

Page 13 / Herb Weitman
Seahawks offensive backfield coach Chick Harris (left) compares the reading of his stopwatch with that of his Raiders counterpart, Ray Willsey, following a 40-yard dash trial.

Page 14 / Ross Lewis
Jets players work out in the weight room of the club's training facility at Hempstead, New York.

Page 15 / Ross Lewis
The heavily muscled arm of a running back displays a brand made with a coat hanger during college days.

Page 16 / Vernon Biever
Under May sunshine in Green Bay, Wisconsin, Packers players participate in a minicamp.

Page 17 / Manny Rubio
The fully equipped weight room of the Atlanta Falcons in the team's training facility at Suwanee, Georgia.

Page 18 / Ross Lewis
The camaraderie of the locker room is one of the pleasurable benefits of offseason workouts at the Jets' Hempstead, New York, training site.

Page 20 / Herb Weitman
Cardinals head coach Jim Hanifan studies a notebook of college prospects as he and the team's personnel people make their decisions regarding available talent during the NFL player draft.

Page 21 / Kevin W. Reece
The final days of April herald a special annual event in the world of the NFL, the selection of eligible college players. The grand ballroom of the Omni Hotel in New York City is the stage as representatives of the 28 clubs and the NFL office conduct the proceedings.

Page 23 / Jim Chaffin
Rams equipment manager Don Hewitt applies decals of the team's famous Rams horns to helmets. On the shelves behind him are helmets from each of the 27 other teams of the NFL.

Page 24 / George Gojkovich
July means the opening of training camps around the NFL. Steelers wide receiver Gregg Garrity walks to a workout at St. Vincent College in Latrobe, Pennsylvania.

Page 25 / Herb Weitman
The teaching tools for the coach—blackboards, movie projectors, screens, and classroom seats.

Training Camp

Pages 28-29 / George Gojkovich
An aerial view of St. Vincent College in Latrobe, Pennsylvania, the site of the Steelers' summer training camp.

Pages 30-31 / John H. Reid III
Veteran Browns offensive tackle Doug Dieken checks into a dormitory at Lakeland Community College in Mentor, Ohio, for his fourteenth—and final—training camp. He retired in April, 1985.

Page 32 / Manny Rubio
Jeff Van Note, 39, the Falcons' most valuable player in 1984 and a five-time NFC Pro Bowl player, anticipates his seventeenth season as Atlanta's center.

Pages 32-33 / Brian Drake
Seahawks head coach Chuck Knox evaluates a July workout at Eastern Washington University in Cheney, Washington.

Page 33 / John E. Biever
Nose tackle Bill Maas, a 6-foot 4-inch, 265-pounder who was the Chiefs' number-one draft choice in 1984, finds a quiet moment at the Kansas City camp at William Jewell College, Liberty, Missouri.

Page 34A / John McDonough
A colorful heavy blocking bag stands ready at the Chargers' training camp at the University of California-San Diego, in La Jolla, California.

Page 97A / Brian Drake
Cowboys quarterback Gary Hogeboom, having paid the price of holding his ground while getting off his pass, spends a dizzying moment on the carpet at Chicago's Soldier Field.

Page 975B / John Biever
Packers head coach Forrest Gregg watches intently as his team engages the Seahawks at Milwaukee County Stadium.

Page 98 / Bill Smith
Against the Bears in Chicago, Lions running back Billy Sims, his eyes already seeking the holes created by his linemen, takes the ball from quarterback Eric Hipple.

Pages 98-99 / Patrick Downs
Saints running back Wayne Wilson is brought to an abrupt halt by Rams safety Johnnie Johnson, left, and linebacker Jim Collins in a game played at Anaheim.

Page 100 / David Boss
Rams cornerback LeRoy Irvin gets a hand in the way of Steve Bartkowski's pass, which is intended for Atlanta Falcons wide receiver Alfred Jenkins.

Page 101 / Rick Stewart
Jim Plunkett, the Raiders' veteran quarterback, shows his displeasure at a failed drive in the Coliseum.

Pages 102-103 / Nate Fine Productions
The attention of the end zone crowd at St. Louis's Busch Stadium is fully engaged as Cardinals kicker Neil O'Donoghue attempts a field goal in a game against the Washington Redskins.

Page 104 / Brian Drake
With time out on the field, Saints trainer Dean Kleinschmidt bends low over guard Brad Edelman during a game at Chicago, trying to determine the severity of an injury.

Page 105 / Michael Zagaris
As linebacker Jack (Hacksaw) Reynolds diagrams plays on a chalkboard, 49ers defensive line coach Bill McPherson points out adjustments to be made in a game against the Patriots at Sullivan Stadium in Foxboro, Massachusetts.

Page 106A / Ross Lewis
As soon as one game is played, another looms ahead in the 16-week NFL schedule. In between, players and coaches prepare with carefully scheduled workouts and meetings. Browns defensive players meet with their coaches to review the offenses they will be seeing on Sunday.

Page 106B / Manny Rubio
Dolphins head coach Don Shula in a chalkboard strategy session with quarterback Dan Marino.

Page 106C / Fred Anderson
With the trees in Eden Prairie, Minnesota, taking on the hues of Indian Summer, the Vikings go through an afternoon workout at the team's facility.

Page 107A / Ross Lewis
A Browns assistant coach shows the fatigue that comes from the long hours of reviewing opponents' game film, charting tendencies, and diagramming new defensive schemes for upcoming games.

Page 107B / Herb Weitman
Cardinals offensive backfield coach Dick Jamieson diagrams plays on the overhead projector during a team meeting.

Page 107C / Walter Iooss, Jr.
A Cowboys player takes heed of Tom Landry's neatly lettered credo and works diligently.

Page 107D / Corky Trewin
A Seahawks assistant trainer gives a massage to running back Curt Warner, easing the stiffness that is a by-product of absorbing some 20 violent tackles per game.

Page 108 / Ross Lewis
Browns cornerback Ron Bolton contemplates his role in the defensive strategy being plotted for the next opponent.

Page 109 / Corky Trewin
Chalk diagrams become animated, full-scale life experiences on Sunday. A camera supported from the center of the Seattle Kingdome's roof captures the precision as Bills quarterback Joe Ferguson sends running back Booker Moore against the Seahawks.

Page 110 / Al Messerschmidt
The hot, near-tropical sun warms Bears running back Walter Payton in Chicago's game against the Buccaneers in Tampa.

Page 111 / Pete J. Groh
Assuming a classic defensive stance, Steelers linebacker Mike Merriweather is ready for action in a game with the Browns at Three Rivers Stadium.

Pages 112-113 / Herb Weitman
Behind the crashing surge of offensive and defensive linemen at Texas Stadium, Cowboys running back Tony Dorsett watches for the opening that will lead him to the Cardinals' goal line.

Pages 114-115 / Peter Read Miller
Rams runner Eric Dickerson is engulfed by 49ers defensive backs Tim Collier and Ronnie Lott in a game played at Anaheim.

Pages 116-117 / John H. Reid III
For NFL athletes, the single thing hardest to accept is defeat. Football is the consummate team game, and success and failure are based on team effort. Chip Banks, the outstanding linebacker for the Cleveland Browns, sheds some tears as his team loses for the seventh time.

Page 117 / Manny Rubio
The spectators at Miami's Orange Bowl join Dolphins wide receiver Mark Clayton in celebration after a touchdown reception of Dan Marino's pass.

Page 118 / Bill Smith
The great runners of pro football often appear to have eyes in the backs of their heads. The Bears' Walter Payton displays that intangible gift as he darts away from a grasping tackler in a game against the Lions at Soldier Field.

Page 119 / George Gojkovich
Pure brute strength is demonstrated by huge Redskins tackle Joe Jacoby as he literally lifts an Eagles opponent away from the play.

Page 120 / John Biever
Vikings defensive end Mark Mullaney (77) and linebacker Fred McNeill pressure Packers quarterback Lynn Dickey at Lambeau Field in Green Bay, Wisconsin.

Page 121 / Peter Read Miller
As a Lions linebacker desperately tries to deflect the ball, Rams tight end Mike Barber makes a reception at Anaheim Stadium.

Page 122 / Peter Read Miller
San Francisco running back Wendell Tyler, attacking the Eagles' goal, is catapulted head over heels by safety Wes Hopkins, with the ball sailing free.

Page 123 / L.D. Fullerton
His one visible eye a dark coal of hot anger, Bengals head coach Sam Wyche makes a strong point to an official during a game against the Oilers at Riverfront Stadium.

Page 124 / Michael Zagaris
Another Sunday, another game? Hardly. Linebacker Todd Shell of the 49ers vomits prior to a game against the Saints at New Orleans's Louisiana Superdome.

Pages 124-125 / Michael Zagaris
"Interminable" is the word that best describes the wait the 49ers must endure in their locker room at Candlestick Park as they listen

for the signal from the referee that will summon them to the field.

Page 126 / David Boss
In San Diego Jack Murphy Stadium, the groundskeepers remove the tarps from the field prior to a Monday night game between the Chargers and the Bears.

Pages 126-127 / Vernon Biever
In a quagmire at Green Bay's Lambeau Field, Packers and Buccaneers flounder in the muck in search of the ball dropped by Buccaneers running back James Wilder.

Pages 128-129 / Corky Trewin
On a Riverfront Stadium field frozen as hard as a skating rink, and with a wet snow falling, Seahawks safety Kenny Easley, with help from linebacker Greg Gaines, tackles Bengals wide receiver Cris Collinsworth.

Page 130 / Dave Stock
For some unfortunate teams, the season can be written off early, yet games still must be played. The Vikings, hopelessly behind late in their game at San Francisco, close out their poorest season in years by attacking the 49ers' goal in one final, futile attempt to score a touchdown.

Page 131 / Al Messerschmidt
A bellowing throng of fans at RFK Stadium watches the Cardinals-Redskins battle for a playoff position on the last Sunday of the regular season. Washington runner John Riggins, often called "The Diesel" for his tireless power, hammers into the heart of the Cardinals' defense.

Page 132 / Dave Stock
49ers tight end Earl Cooper spikes the football following a score against the Rams as San Francisco celebrates winning another NFC Western Division title.

Page 133 / Jay Dickman
After a brilliantly played, but losing, Monday night game against the Dolphins in Miami's Orange Bowl, disappointed Cowboys coach Tom Landry leaves the field, his team eliminated from the playoffs for the first time in more than a decade.

Page 134A / Scott Cunningham
Following a game in Anaheim, Falcons running back William Andrews hugs Rams offensive coordinator Jimmy Raye, who had been Andrews's offensive coach at Atlanta two seasons earlier.

Page 134B / Nate Fine Productions
Redskins head coach Joe Gibbs is joined by quarterback coach Jerry Rhome as they happily leave the field at RFK Stadium with another Washington victory.

Page 134C / Bob and Sylvia Allen
Brothers Keith (57) and Joey Browner meet after a game between their teams, the Buccaneers and the Vikings, at Tampa Stadium. A third brother, Ross, plays for the Cincinnati Bengals.

Page 134D / Rick Stewart
Two record-setting NFL running backs meet in the postgame period at Anaheim Stadium. The Bears' Walter Payton congratulates the Rams' Eric Dickerson on Los Angeles's victory.

Page 134E / George Gojkovich
With dusk falling, groundskeepers clean up at Cleveland Stadium following a November game with Cincinnati.

Page 135 / George Gojkovich
Denver's youthful quarterback John Elway shows his joy as his team wins the AFC Western Division championship.

Tournament

Page 138 / George Gojkovich
The message of the playoffs is carried in the glare of Steelers defensive end Keith Gary.

Page 139 / Jim Chaffin
Raiders defensive end Howie Long leads his teammates onto the field.

Page 140 / George Gojkovich
Broncos head coach Dan Reeves has something to say to quarterback John Elway, who is reflected in Reeves's glasses.

Page 141 / Al Messerschmidt
Steelers rookie Rich Erenberg returns the opening kickoff of an AFC Championship Game against Miami. Mike Kozlowski makes the tackle.

Page 142A / Manny Rubio
Bears defensive tackle Dan Hampton stalks Redskins quarterback Joe Theismann in an NFC divisional playoff game at RFK Stadium.

Page 142B / Allan Kaye
Cowboys quarterback Danny White, a veteran of playoff games, reflects the tension of a championship contest.

Page 143A / Al Messerschmidt
Dolphins quarterback Dan Marino, able to see clearly through a jumble of scrambling players, passes against the Seahawks in a playoff game at the Orange Bowl.

Page 143B / Manny Rubio
Walter Payton finds a wide hole in the Redskins' defense.

Page 143C / Dave Stock
49ers linebacker Riki Ellison flies toward a ball fumbled by Giants running back Rob Carpenter in a playoff game at Candlestick Park.

Page 144A / John McDonough
Dolphins defensive end Doug Betters battles New York Jets tackle Marvin Powell.

Page 144B / Arthur Anderson
Referee Gene Barth, right, engages in a discussion with fellow officials Dean Look, left, and Ron Botchan, during a game between the 49ers and the Giants at Candlestick Park.

Page 144C / Bill Cummings
Giants inside linebacker Harry Carson shows rage and frustration during a playoff game against the 49ers.

Page 145 / Amos Love
The pure athletic grace of Raiders running back Marcus Allen is evident as he races 49 yards for a touchdown in a game against Pittsburgh at the Los Angeles Coliseum.

Page 146 / Peter Read Miller
Wide receiver Dwight Clark hugs 49ers teammate Freddie Solomon (88) following a touchdown catch against the Bears in an NFC Championship Game at Candlestick Park.

Page 147 / Peter Read Miller
The tattered and bloodied arm of Raiders inside linebacker Matt Millen tells its own story.

Page 148 / Amos Love
Ignoring the message board at Candlestick Park, San Francisco fans dig up divots of painted turf as souvenirs of another 49ers title.

Page 149A / Peter Read Miller
In a deserted locker room, Jack Youngblood, a 14-year defensive end for the Rams, finishes dressing following a playoff loss to the Giants.

Page 149B / Herb Weitman
St. Louis coach Jim Hanifan, alone with thoughts of a season that ended all too abruptly.

Super Bowl

Page 152 / Michael Zagaris
In typical Super Bowl week fashion, mobs of reporters create small islands on the field at Candlestick Park, seeking quotes and back-

ground information for their stories. In the foreground, 49ers corner-back Ronnie Lott holds the attention of a media group.

Page 153 / Al Messerschmidt
One of the toughest parts of Super Bowl week for players and coaches is the hours spent answering the questions of the media. Quarterback Joe Montana of the 49ers draws a crowd in a session at Candlestick Park.

Page 154A / Michael Zagaris
On the Friday before the Super Bowl, it is customary for NFL Commissioner Pete Rozelle to hold a press conference to comment and answer questions on all aspects of the state of professional football.

Page 154B / Al Messerschmidt
To provide comfort to the 84,069 spectators at Super Bowl XIX, Apple Computer of nearby Cupertino, California, provided brightly covered souvenir cushions to cover the plank-style seating at Stanford Stadium.

Page 154C / Corky Trewin
George Toma, the groundskeeper for Super Bowl, removes a tarp covering the surface at Stanford Stadium.

Page 154D / Dave Cross
Dolphins coach Don Shula holds an impromptu seminar for ABC-TV's broadcast team on the morning of Super Bowl XIX. Frank Gifford, Joe Theismann, and Don Meredith listen attentively.

Page 155 / Baron Wolman
On Saturday afternoon, a baseball game commences quietly on the grounds of Stanford University, while the campus is transformed by several specially erected corporate-sponsor tents, creating a small, temporary city beside the stadium.

Page 156A / Corky Trewin
Artist LeRoy Nieman sketches as the San Francisco 49ers take their pregame warmups.

Page 156B / Michael Zagaris
Cornerback Ronnie Lott of the 49ers has his ankles taped before the big game. The wear and tear of a long 22-week season is registered clearly by the additional tape wrapping his body.

Page 156C / Michael Zagaris
The 49ers' quarterbacks and kickers wait quietly before their lockers at Super Bowl XIX: Quarterbacks Joe Montana and Matt Cavanaugh, punter Max Runager, and kicker Ray Wersching.

Page 157A / Rob Brown
Outside, early arriving spectators are entertained by colorful pre-game musical programs. The St. Louis Cardinals' Huddles mascot gets into the spirit of things with a Super Bowl XIX cheerleader.

Page 157B / Peter Read Miller
As kickoff approaches, thousands of balloons are released.

Page 157C / Bob Barnes
Coach Bill Walsh of the 49ers waits outside the 49ers' locker room, lost in thought as photographer Bob Allen snaps some pictures.

Page 158 / Richard Mackson
Wide receiver Dwight Clark of the 49ers awaits his introduction.

Page 159A / Michael Zagaris
Former 49ers star and Pro Football Hall of Fame running back Hugh McElhenny conducts the coin flip ceremonies at Super Bowl XIX. President Ronald Reagan made the actual toss at the White House over television.

Page 159B / Alan Schwartz
The Dolphins display high spirits.

Pages 160-161 / Manny Rubio
At midfield, 49ers running back Roger Craig (33) follows the block of guard Randy Cross (51) as San Francisco challenges the Dolphins' defense.

Page 162A / Richard Mackson
The body language of Dolphins coach Don Shula and back-up quarterback Don Strock indicates how the game on the field is going for the Dolphins.

Page 162B / Michael Zagaris
Fred Dean, the 49ers' sack specialist, has a hand-painted message on his shoes.

Page 163 / Richard Mackson
The arm of 49ers quarterback Joe Montana is ready to fire another pass downfield as Dolphins and 49ers players maneuver around him.

Pages 164-165 / Richard Mackson
With a damp ground fog covering the field late in the game at Stanford Stadium, the Dolphins' huge offensive linemen puff steam.

Page 166 / Al Messerschmidt
Following a six-yard touchdown run, 49ers quarterback Joe Montana, embraced by running back Roger Craig, reaches out to share his joy with close friend and teammate Dwight Clark.

Page 167 / George Gojkovich
With the outcome no longer in doubt, Dolphins quarterback Dan Marino, 23, absorbs the reality of a Super Bowl defeat while pondering the inevitable "what-if?" questions.

Page 168A / Corky Trewin
Coach Bill Walsh of the 49ers is given a victory ride from the field.

Page 168B / Michael Zagaris
Their job completed and a second Super Bowl victory in four years a reality, the 49ers' veteran offensive linemen gather near their bench for a sideline portrait (left to right: offensive line coach Bobb McKittrick, center Fred Quillan, guard Randy Cross, tackles Bubba Paris and Keith Fahnhorst, and guard John Ayers. Tight end Earl Cooper [89] stands behind them).

Page 169 / Michael Zagaris
In the San Francisco locker room, NFL Commissioner Pete Rozelle awards the Vince Lombardi Trophy to the Super Bowl champion 49ers. Head coach Bill Walsh and owner Edward DeBartolo, Jr., accept as ABC-TV's Jim Lampley holds the microphone.

Front Endsheets / Herb Weitman
Tools to measure a National Football League game: The 10-yard-long chain markers, the drive-start marker, the opposite-side bulls-eye marker (which moves when the 10-yard chain marker moves), and the four-downs indicator.

Rear Endsheets / Manny Rubio
On a rainy night in Georgia, an NFL game between the Falcons and Rams is broadcast to a nation of viewers.